God created healthy things for our body.

Circle the healthy foods.

God created us to enjoy life!

Jesus said, "I am the Bread of Life." John 6:35

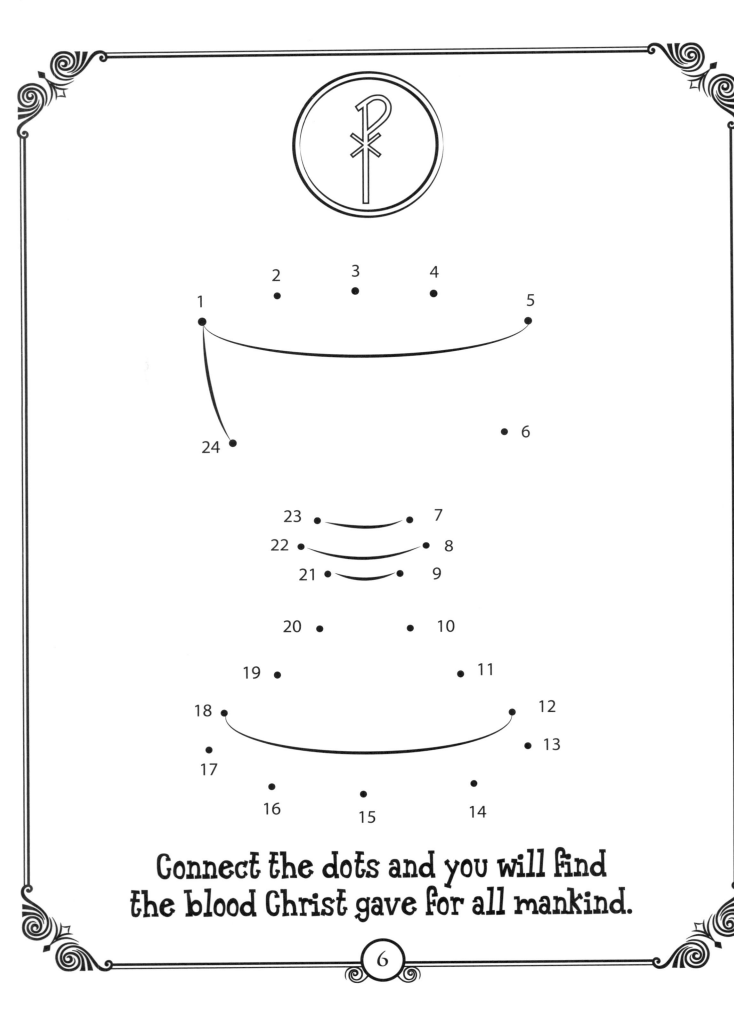

Connect the dots and you will find
the blood Christ gave for all mankind.

God cares for our souls.

Jesus is the Bread of Life!

Match the shadows.

Answer key is on the inside back cover

Imelda was a little girl
that wanted to serve God.

# Jesus answered Imelda's prayers!

# Help Imelda make her way to the altar.

# Just like Imelda, Brother Francis loves Jesus!

Jesus wants to be close to you, too!

# The Eucharist is a celebration!
(Fill in the happy faces.)